BL... TO TAX

A.J. CARROLL

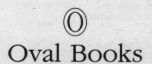

Oval Books

Published by Oval Books
335 Kennington Road
London SE11 4QE
United Kingdom

Telephone: +44 (0)20 7582 7123
Fax: +44 (0)20 7582 1022
E-mail: info@ovalbooks.com
Web site: www.ovalbooks.com

First published by Ravette Publishing, 1997
First published by Oval Books, 2000

New Edition 2004

Series Editor – Anne Tauté

Cover designer – Rob Oliver
Cover image – © Masterfile/Zefa
Printer – Cox & Wyman Ltd.
Producer – Oval Projects Ltd.

The Bluffer's® Guides series is based
on an original idea by Peter Wolfe.

The Bluffer's Guide®, The Bluffer's Guides®,
Bluffer's®, and Bluff Your Way® are
Registered Trademarks.

The author and The Bluffer's® Guides
disclaim responsibility for all consequences of
any person acting on, or refraining from acting
on, the information contained in this book
including negligence, utter reliance, or the
need for an artificial stimulant.

ISBN-13: 978-1-903096-75-8
ISBN-10: 1-903096-75-8

CONTENTS

INTRODUCTION

Tax is a game. Like most other games it is played between two teams, in this case The Taxman v. the Rest of the World.

It has both written and unwritten rules, which have to be learnt by both sides. There are referees, such as the Parliamentary Ombudsman and the European Court of Justice. Some games are quiet local matches with no-one turning out except the players. Others are televised and reported world-wide. Players can be off-side or sent off, like Lester Piggott, Nissan U.K., and Steffi Graff's Dad.

The pitch markings for the game are unclear, so neither side knows how to behave in the grey areas around the edges. This makes it more interesting for good players.

Tax is also played on many levels, like a computer game, so experts can travel through income tax and personal allowances to the highest levels of international tax. But one wrong move may mean relegation to a lower division.

Unwillingly and unwittingly, you too are a player in this game. This guide will help you to keep control, rather than trip over the ball. It may also help you understand what happens to the money you give away every day to people you have never met.

THE BASICS

Most governments regard people as sheep, who are fleeced regularly by taxes. The aim is: maximum wool, minimum bleating. If you become an effective tax bluffer, you are less likely to have this wool pulled over your eyes. The first step is to grasp the basics: what is taxed, why, and how.

What

Food, drink, income, capital, petrol, pensions, dying, betting, telephones and rubbish are all taxed, but this complexity can be reduced to a few basic principles. Tax is really only charged on three things:

1. **Bodies**, whether dead or alive, as in Death Duties or Poll Tax.

2. **Assets**, including money, land and houses.

3. **Transactions**, such as buying and selling.

This abbreviates as **BAT**, and helps to explain the widespread fear of flying mammals. Tax systems really suck your blood.

Why

The truth is, a great deal of taxpayers' money has always been frittered away on ill-designed projects or amusements. But because it is dangerous and insensitive for rulers to admit this, they have always bluffed.

In the old days, taxes were to pay for war, to keep the peace or to protect the people from Saladin or the

Tzar of Russia. Today, their bluff is more sophisticated. Tax is a necessary good, providing funding for a whole range of social benefits. It also has a secondary use, as a psychological weapon, a form of aversion therapy. Governments impose heavy taxes on some behaviour, such as smoking and drinking, but reward desirable actions – like getting married or giving to charity – with tax relief.

What is encouraged or discouraged changes over time. In the 1930s, the German fiscal system supported people with children; conversely, if a Chinese couple break the 'one child' policy, two years' earnings may be taken in tax.

How

All taxes are either **direct** or **indirect***. Direct tax hits you between the eyes. Income tax and capital gains tax are direct taxes. Indirect tax is like living on a plateau: you tend to forget you are not at sea level. Without realising it, you pay a base level of indirect taxes as part of everyday costs.

Occasionally indirect taxes *are* noticeable, like mountain peaks rising from the plains. This is when the cost increase is particularly high, such as duties on tobacco, perfume, and alcohol. Even then the peak is only really noticeable when you go abroad, and realise how cheap the wine is.

---

* The Inland Revenue have traditionally been responsible for assessing direct taxes, while indirect taxes have been left to Customs. The Treasury is now bringing both arms together – an attempt to let the right hand see what the left is doing. Bluffers might like to emulate Edward Troup, an eminent tax lawyer, and refer to the newly merged body as 'Finance Collection UK'.

THE FAMOUS FIVE

Most tax systems have five main characters, without whom it is difficult to write a script at all. There are also a host of minor parts. Some players appear in disguise, while others are on stage for such a long time that the audience thinks they are part of the scenery. Some are hated villains, to be booed off the stage, like the Poll Tax. Others are everyday soap-opera taxes such as VAT. But the five star performers are taxes on **income**, **corporations**, **capital gains**, **sales** and **death**.

Income Tax

Income tax is paid mostly by individuals, and is a tax on income, rather than capital.

The classic distinction between capital and income is that capital is the 'tree' and income is the 'fruit'. But this is simplistic: everyone can tell an oak from an apple. It is more difficult to know whether a pile of money has come from capital growth or income. Mentioning this to tax specialists will earn you their grudging respect.

The main thing to remember in practice is that capital growth is easier to shelter from tax than income, and thus generally to be preferred.

Income tax is almost invariably banded. The names for each band will vary by country, as will their number, but the same basic principle appears almost everywhere. For example, in the U.K. people with very little income pay no tax at all because it is covered by **allowances**, such as the personal allowance. The next income group also pay no tax on this first slice, and pay **lower rate** tax on the next.

Most people fall into the third group, and are known as **basic rate** taxpayers. The top slice of their income is taxed at the basic rate. **Higher rate** taxpayers form the fourth and final group, and they pay all three rates of tax. Remember that top rate tax is only charged on the last slice.

A useful practical point is that the **self-employed** pay less tax than employees, given the same level of income. This is because employees are the only group in society against whom it is still legal to discriminate. Different governments have different methods, but they all discriminate.

It is, of course, easier to collect taxes from people with a regular salary than from the self-employed whose affairs are always more delicate. In some countries, such as Greece, almost all income tax is paid by government employees.

In the U.K., the discrimination is twofold: benefits and deductions.

Benefits

Employees may be given non-cash benefits such as company cars and health insurance. Although benefits used to save tax, a combination of new laws and inflation means that it is the taxman who now gets the benefit.

Company cars, in particular, have been targeted by legislation. Knowing this fact gives you a powerful weapon. In any business meeting mention that, as company cars are no longer tax-efficient, you have heard they will soon be replaced by a cash allowance. Most executives are so attached to their cars that you will thus be able to deflect any meeting from its original objective.

A staff Christmas party is an excellent benefit for professional bluffers. But beware, if an employer is too generous, the costs of your food, drink, entertainment and mini-cab home will all appear on your tax return. Scrooge is a seasonal tradition too.

There are numerous other so-called benefits, all of which have to logged by employers on a Form P11D. Since the Inland Revenue gets a copy there is no point in bluffing: just check that the form is right before using it to help complete your tax return.

Should the Inland Revenue suggest you should be paying tax on some new benefit, such as:

- using the firm's photocopiers to duplicate your Christmas letters
- 'borrowing' office stationery for use at home
- calling a cousin in New York on the office phone

remind the official that there is a real world outside, and that keeping records for this type of benefit is ridiculous. The magic word here is **deregulation**. The U.K. government regularly promises that it will cut red tape for business. It should never be allowed to forget this.

Deductions

In Britain the self-employed can deduct expenses from their taxable income if the costs are 'wholly and exclusively' for business reasons. This means that a **dual purpose** expense cannot be claimed.

Mallalieu v. Drummond is the seminal tax case here. It is one of two tax cases suitable for discussing at dinner parties. The other is *CIR v. Aken* (q.v.).

Ms. Mallalieu was a barrister who, like other barristers, was required to wear black in court. She always wore coloured clothes at home, so she claimed a tax deduction for her court dress. However the House of Lords decided the black clothes were not wholly and exclusively for work, but partly to 'preserve warmth and decency'. In other words, she could not go naked to court. This would have made her guilty of conduct liable to cause a breach of the peace.

Mallalieu is an extreme example. Surprisingly, the Revenue does recognise the division of some expenses. For example, if you work from home, you can claim tax relief on part of your heating bills, not to mention repairs to your waterworks.

If costs exceed income, you may have a **tax loss**, which could work in your favour if you:

a) offset it against other taxable income, such as bank interest,

b) carry it forward to reduce next year's taxable profits, or,

c) carry it back against last year's profits.

Individual tax losses are a bluffer's delight. Can you convince the Revenue that your expensive hobby is a loss-making business, and thus reduce your over-all tax bill? To succeed you will need to show you tried to make profits, but if you make losses for too many years, the Inspector will call your bluff.

Some hobbies meet more resistance than others. A classic non-starter is buying and selling shares. In *Salt v. Chamberlain* the taxpayer was a mathematician with computer skills, who systematically dealt on the stock exchange. However his system was unsuccessful, and he made losses. The court held he was not trading and therefore could not claim loss relief. Had he succeeded, the Revenue would have been inundated by similar sob stories.

Employees have to meet a more stringent test for expenses. Their costs must be 'wholly, exclusively and necessarily' spent in carrying out their work. Adding this one word, 'necessarily', makes the test almost impossible to meet. It means, 'necessary for everyone who does a similar job'. Thus, while you may need to buy the *Financial Times* or *Racing Post* every day to understand your clients' business, you will only get a tax deduction for the cost if it would be impossible to do your job without it ('No F.T., no comment').

The solution can be stage managed: get your employer to purchase what you need and give it to you. If he buys the newspaper and lets you read it, his cost is deductible because employers do not need to pass the 'necessary' test. The Revenue relies on their parsimony.

Corporate Tax

A company is a separate person in law and thus has a **legal personality**. It is therefore treated as an entity distinct from the shareholders who own it, and from the employees and directors who work for it. This separation is known as the **corporate veil**. Company law does not normally permit outsiders to lift this veil, although it can be renounced voluntarily, as in 'The Dance of the Seven...' In exchange for this privileged modesty, a company pays its own taxes.

Profits

Companies are generally taxed on their profits. The point to note is that **taxable profits** are often different from accounting profits. This is because:

a) Accounts contain round sum estimates, and these estimates are hated by tax gatherers. They like to pretend tax is an exact science, like economics.

b) Tax law requires that some amounts are calculated in a special way for tax purposes.

c) Some expenses are specifically forbidden for tax purposes. In certain countries, for example, customer entertaining is **disallowed** – a suitable excuse, if you are the host, for not buying the next round.

You therefore cannot simply take the accounting profit and multiply it by the tax rate. That would be far too straightforward.

Losses

If a company makes **taxable losses** rather than profits, **tax reliefs** provide a consolation prize for shareholders. The rules vary by country, but generally a loss can be used to reduce some or all of the following:

- Future taxable profits of the company.

- Past taxable profits of the company. This is better than the first option because you recover tax paid in earlier years, sometimes with interest.

- Taxable profits of other companies owned by the same shareholders. For this to be possible, the tax system must treat such companies as a group for tax purposes. These are known as **group relief** provisions, and are necessary if you want to play premier league tax games.

Tax losses thus have their uses. If you are responsible for the loss in the first place, knowing this may save your bacon.

Small and Close

There are two interesting corporate tax variants: **small** companies and **close** companies. Some are small and some are close. Some very cuddly ones are both small and close.

Close companies are ones with relatively few shareholders. Special, complex tax rules apply to them, and these can safely be left to the experts; bluffers need only ensure that they call them 'close', not 'closed'.

Small companies are ones that have relatively low profits and turnover, and the rate of tax paid is less than that suffered by large companies – in some cases it is as low as 0%. If you are involved with a company, make sure that it is being taxed at the correct rate – you might be overpaying.

In the United States, small companies are known as 'S Corporations'. These are See-through for tax purposes, in that the shareholders' corporate veil is transparent.

Dividends

Company profits are first taxed and then paid out to shareholders as dividends. These are then taxed in the hands of the shareholders.

This double bounce troubled the conscience of some taxmen who, in an unexpected burst of compassion, invented a complicated **imputation system** to prevent the same income being taxed twice. Examples are the *avoir fiscal* in France and, in Britain, **Advance Corporation Tax** – abbreviated as ACT, pronounced A-Sea-Tea, and not 'act' as in 'double-act'. However recent U.K. Governments first reduced this relief to a mere shadow of its former self, and then abolished it altogether.

Capital Gains Tax

In the beginning there was income tax, but it was too easy to avoid. For example, companies pay their profits to shareholders as dividends, which are taxed as income. If no dividend is paid, profits accumulate within the company. The shares will reflect this accumulated value, which could be realised on a sale. Income could thus be converted into a tax-free capital gain. A open goal of this sort could not be allowed. The Revenue's counter-offensive was **capital gains tax (CGT)**.

Gains can be either **realised** or **unrealised**. If you sell an asset at a profit, this is a realised gain. If the asset has gone up in value, but has not been sold, you have an unrealised gain. Such an asset can be described as 'pregnant with gains'. It means that gains exist but have not yet been delivered.

In general, capital gains taxes only bite when there is a realised gain. This is for the good practical reason that otherwise you may have no cash to pay the tax.

Exemption

Never make the mistake of thinking that all assets are subject to CGT. Some are too trivial to bother with, such as low value antiques. Others, such as cars, are almost invariably sold at a loss, and the Revenue wants to prevent people accumulating tax losses. Decorations for gallantry are excluded because taxing them would be bad form.

Small gains, up to an annual tax-free amount, are often excluded from tax. This is because the tax is so horribly complicated, even the Revenue do not want to work out the sums.

So find out the annual exemption, and keep your gains below it. This way you never pay.

Avoiding Taxable Gains

If your gains are going to be above the limit, consider:

1. **Realising losses**. If you own other assets which are now worth less than when you bought them (i.e. have **unrealised losses**), contemplate selling them and realising the losses. This allows you to offset the losses against your gains, reducing your total taxable amount.

2. **Spouse exemption**. Your spouse has a tax-free amount too, and gifts of assets to one another are not taxed. If you give some of the assets to your spouse and he/she sells them, this will use up his/her tax-free allowance, not yours.

   There are a number of points to watch here:
   - You can only transfer assets, not gains. So if you have already sold the assets, it's too late.
   - Your spouse has to sell the assets freely and must be able to keep the money. If you require him/her to sell, or the money goes into your bank account, the Revenue may challenge the transfer as a fake.
   - If your marriage is under strain, transfers are dicey. A gift of several thousand pounds may improve the relationship, but equally it may fund your spouse's clandestine assignations.

3. **Bed and breakfast**. In tax terms this means selling shares at the end of one day and buying them back first thing the next. If you have unrealised losses, but want to go on owning the shares, bed and breakfasting allows you to realise the loss, but hang on to the asset.

   Unfortunately, bed and breakfasting is regarded as the tax equivalent of a dirty weekend. Legislation now makes it more difficult to consummate the arrangement. If you've sold your shares you cannot buy them back for 30 days if you want the same tax benefit. Because the price may move during the month, this is like spending four weeks 'on business' in the Caribbean – there is a far greater risk of being found out.

One solution is to sell the shares to your spouse. This remains legal. It is, after all, morally right that husbands and wives share each other's bed and breakfast.

Calculating Gains

If you are finding your CGT position difficult, be grateful. You are rich beyond most people's wildest dreams. Employ a professional, and keep him on his toes by asking if he has considered:

- **Losses**. These can be set against gains, effectively increasing the total tax-free amount.

- **Transaction costs**. Most costs of buying and selling the asset are allowable for tax.

- **Enhancement costs**. If you paid over the odds when you installed CCTV security or attached a conservatory to your holiday home, console yourself by claiming tax relief on their cost.

- **Taper Relief**. This was supposed to simplify the tax system and discourage short-termism, and you should be cynical about both. With taper relief, the longer you hold an asset, the smaller your gain and the less tax you pay. However the gain stops shrinking after a maximum of ten years, which makes it easier for those who count on their fingers.

The fairy tale answer – a negligible rate of tax – applies if you own 'business assets'. But it is difficult to squeeze into these rules. As in the pantomime, the silver slipper often doesn't fit, and you can end up with the ugly sister. What is more, the taxman has a box of conjuring tricks which turn business assets into pumpkins in a flash.

Value Added and Sales Tax

VAT is a chain letter. This is how it works:

1. A forester cuts down a tree, sells the wood to a carpenter, and adds VAT to the sale price.

2. The carpenter makes a bookcase, adding VAT to his sale price. The key point to remember is that he doesn't pay all this VAT to the government. He first deducts the tax he paid the woodcutter when he bought the wood. Hence the tax he pays is only on the value he has added to the wood. (Note that this applies even if no value has been added, such as repairing an antique).

3. The chain continues, from carpenter to distributor, from distributor to shopkeeper. Each pays some VAT.

4. But all chain letters have a victim, usually the unsuspecting man in the street. VAT is no different. The one who buys the bookcase and takes it home pays tax on the full cost, and can deduct nothing.

Sales taxes in many countries operate in exactly the same way. In some the system is less sophisticated, with tax only charged at the final stage, the sale to the consumer. But even then their similarities to VAT are greater than their differences. In particular:

- Both are **regressive**: the less you earn, the bigger the share of your income it takes. This is the opposite of income taxes, which are **progressive**.

- Both are **indirect taxes**, making leakage from wallets less obvious. This is why they are favoured by governments which have an impossible programme of tax cuts: they reduce the **headline rate** of direct tax, while indirect taxes are surreptitiously notched up.

- Both are collected by business people who are press-ganged into being unpaid VAT collectors. Don't ever underestimate the amount of time the paperwork takes. It is the sting in the tail of self-employment.

One of the problems with VAT is that it does not apply to everything. Each country has at least two rates, and deciding which rate applies keeps Eurocrats' minds fully exercised. In the U.K., although food has a zero rate of VAT, some particularly delicious edibles are not classified as food, but as luxuries. So biscuits are food, but chocolate isn't. Thus assorted biscuits count as food provided they have less than 15% chocolate content – which is why there are never enough chocolate biscuits in the tin.

There are also some goods and services, such as banking and insurance, which are exempt from VAT. It is very easy to go wrong at this point, by assuming that exemption is a good thing. Normally it is. If you are exempt from corporation tax or CGT, you don't pay it. But VAT is different: if you are exempt from

VAT you cannot charge VAT to your customers. But you still have to pay VAT to your suppliers, and will not be allowed to recover it.

Care is also needed to distinguish exemption from zero-rating. If you manufacture plain biscuits, they are zero rated, and you do not have to charge VAT when you sell them. However you can also reclaim all the VAT that was included in your purchases. Thus, instead of paying VAT, Customs will send you a tax refund. This is the ideal position, and the complete opposite of being exempt.

Small businesses with a low turnover do not need to charge VAT at all. This is a good thing, but an audacious bluffer may do even better. If you are selling zero-rated goods, **voluntary registration** allows you to reclaim the VAT suffered on your purchases. Freely agreeing to come within a tax sounds risky, but it is no more dangerous than the eyes on a butterfly's wing. You recover money from Customs, and administration is your only cost.

Death Duties

Death duties, like death itself, have many euphemisms – Inheritance Tax (**IHT**), Estate Duty, Probate Duty and Capital Transfer Tax. But they all mean the same. It is the Revenue's revenge for reducing the taxpaying population.

Dead people can't complain or vote and so are easy to tax. The Roman Emperor Augustus was the first to realise this. He sent tax collectors to the homes of the newly deceased to pick over their possessions. The collectors stamped '*Requiescat in pace*' or R.I.P., on anything they did not fancy, and beneficiaries had to settle for the left-overs.

In most tax systems part of the deceased's possessions can still be passed on without tax. For example, in many countries bequests to spouses are partly or wholly tax free. Small estates also escape, for a very practical reason: the tax costs too much to collect.

The combination of death and taxes worries people. Don't be thrown by it. Inheritance planning is difficult; after all, only suicides know the key date, and few people are prepared to go to such lengths even to save tax. In any case, most inheritance tax schemes are invalidated by suicide, because otherwise they would be too easy to effect.

Serious inheritance tax planning involves complicated legal webs woven to trap some of the deceased's money and prevent it falling into the taxman's hands. Some schemes manage this – most of the money ends up in the hands of the lawyers.

Such complexity may be more trouble than it's worth, unless you are very rich. Most bluffers only need to consider:

1. Being generous now. Gifts made by the living are partly or wholly tax free.

2. Buying a life insurance policy to fund death duties.

3. Leaving everything above the exempt amount to your spouse. This is tax free because it is thought that, even with a significant financial incentive, married people will not kill each other. Sometimes this optimism is misplaced.

4. Staying alive as long as possible, thus delaying collection of the tax.

21

MINOR CHARACTERS

National Insurance Contributions

In the U.K. the most interesting minor player is itself a bluffer. National Insurance Contributions (**NIC**) is an income tax disguised as an entitlement to state benefits.

Under NIC you pay 'contributions', and receive in turn various allowances, payable when times are hard – if you lose your job, fall ill, or become pregnant. In reality the link is very slight. The word 'contribution' is particularly misleading, implying as it does that the tax is voluntary.

There are several types of NIC, some paid by employers, and others by employees. The self-employed have two specific classes, while benefits such as company cars have a sub-class all to themselves.

NICs are ignored by many tax specialists as beneath their dignity, and you may wish to follow their example. However, they can come in useful at difficult meetings about salary and benefit changes. The simple question, 'How will this change affect the NIC position?' trips up most personnel managers and allows employees time to regroup.

Property Taxes

These are also known as taxes on **real property**. It would be reasonable to think this name reflects the fact that houses are tangible measures of wealth. In fact real means 'fixed', as distinct from property which can be carried around in a briefcase.

An Englishman's home may be his castle, but he still has to pay council tax on it – and possibly business rates as well. Local property taxes tend to be crude, and have always been based on rough estimations of value. In an earlier century property values were estimated by counting the windows. Bricking them up was commonplace, condemning residents to the gloom of a shady tax avoidance scheme.

Stamp Duty

Stamp duty is a tax on documents, not on philately. It is a simple and ancient tax, first introduced in 1694. You pay your tax and your document is stamped by the Controller of Stamps.

If a transaction involves no documents, there is no tax. This suggests that stamp duty is optional, because it can be avoided by simply doing without the document. However the sanction lies elsewhere: only stamped documents can be produced as evidence of ownership in a court of law. So if you ever need to prove title to your shares, stamping the document stops the other side calling your bluff.

Stamp duty used to apply to shares and property. But there is now a new, tougher tax on property deals called **Stamp Duty Land Tax**. SDLT is stamp duty with teeth. It has to be paid even when there is no document, and whether or not the seller and purchaser are in the U.K. It has thus succeeded where generations of Inspectors have failed – it has stamped out Britain's oldest tax avoidance scheme.

Be careful not to confuse SDLT with SDRT. SDRT is **Stamp Duty Reserve Tax**, an obscure levy which replaces stamp duty on some transactions such as unit trusts. It is often hidden in the small print of fund management charges. Asking your financial adviser "What about the SDRT?" may encourage a less reserved approach to fiscal transparency.

Other Taxes

Airport taxes are widespread. Like most indirect taxes, they slip insidiously into the cost, and only the most alert travellers notice their increased ticket price.

Cars are heavily taxed almost everywhere, as is **fuel**. As so many goods need to travel by road, these taxes feed through into the price of goods. So a bicycle is only partly effective as a tax-avoidance device.

To encourage recycling, **landfill taxes** are levied on those who dump rubbish, such as chemical companies, rubble removers and tree surgeons. Garbage is classified and then taxed by weight (though there is a special exemption for burying pets). Evading this tax is expensive as there is no upper limit on the penalty. Customs believe that where there's muck there's money.

Some countries have **net worth taxes**. In France the super-rich have to pay tax based on a percentage of their total wealth. This is a small cost compared to the other taxes they are doubtless avoiding: how else do they remain so rich?

TAX RELIEFS

Like the original 'good news, bad news' joke, governments commonly impose tax with one hand and take it away with the other.

If you ever undress a tax adviser, you will find tax reliefs up his sleeve. These are produced like a dramatic conjuring trick, usually shortly after he tells you his chargeable hourly rate.

You may be unusually lucky and qualify for **quick succession relief**, a reduction in the inheritance tax payable if a person's death is quickly followed by that of a beneficiary. But this is relatively uncommon: few people die from a surfeit of pleasure. **Rollover relief** is more likely. This allows you to roll the gain you have made selling one asset into another. The secret of success is never to let the gap between one disposal and the next acquisition be too long – a simple feat for anyone practised in the art of serial relationships.

Holdover relief is more temporary than rollover relief. After a certain period it wears off. This is especially true if a **wasting asset** is involved, which, regrettably, it all too often is. In tax terms a wasting asset is one which diminishes naturally, such as a lease.

If it all became too exhausting, the over-50s used to be able to claim **retirement relief**. This allowed them to dispose of their businesses, while paying little or no tax. The government has now pensioned off this tax break, arguing that it is non-PC for the fiscal system to discriminate on the basis of age. (They need the increased tax to pay your pensions).

Each country has its own system of tax reliefs. It is possible to do a round-the-world tax-relief tour, but before you set out check the latest tax agents' updates. Recommendations include:

- Procreating in France, with its 'nursery to university' child-related reliefs.
- Being mean in the U.S., which taxes many gifts.
- Buying a tax-deductible wardrobe in Japan, after an earthquake has swallowed the first.
- Falling ill in Germany, where the costs are allowable.
- Dying in Italy, where tax relief can be claimed on your funeral.

25

In reality some reliefs are so small as to be an embarrassment. The U.K. gives a tiny tax allowance to the blind. New Zealand has a housekeeper allowance which will just about cover the cost of a week's tea and biscuits. Germany allows a scarcely visible deduction for church taxes and charitable donations.

At the other end of the scale, **capital allowances** are an important tax relief. Most tax systems have capital allowances, a.k.a. '**tax depreciation**'. Key facts are:

- They are available on **capital assets**, broadly those with an expected life of at least two years.

- A percentage of the purchase cost can be deducted from taxable income for each year you use the asset in your business. The percentage is almost invariably set by the government, though ships have '**free depreciation**', so their owners can choose how much to deduct each year. This generosity stops them sailing away to a better tax regime.

- Allowances can be claimed on industrial buildings (IBAs), agricultural buildings (ABAs), and plant and machinery. ABAs apply to barns, sheds, farm shops, cottages, fences and one-third of your farmhouse (happily the taxman doesn't want to know what happens in the other two-thirds.

  IBAs can only be claimed on buildings which could have existed at the time of Queen Victoria, such as mills, factories, canals, tunnels, bridges and tea plantations, plus shelters for cereal-threshers and ploughmen.

  All attempts to bring these tax reliefs out of the 19th century to cover offices, banks, or retail shops have been rejected. It would make them both too expensive and too useful.

Plant and machinery allowances are more widely available than IBAs and also more generous. The Revenue thus has an even greater incentive to reduce claims, but has to rely on its own initiative rather than the legislation. Its chief weapon is 'self assessment', a confessional tax system under which you cough up your own tax liability.

Hundreds of cases on capital allowances have come to court. Many tell you little about tax but a lot about taxpayers' persistence and ingenuity. For example, the Revenue have succeeded in proving that stallions, wallpaper pattern books, floating restaurants, quarantine kennels, and inflatable tennis court covers are *not* plant and machinery.

On the other hand, detailed analysis of almost any building will produce a list of hidden assets which are allowable. Hot water pipes, lavatories, basins, lifts and moveable partitions are all eligible. If you want to unsettle a property manager or tax accountant, ask if he's comfortable that all available capital allowances have been claimed. Then sit back and watch him squirm.

Playing House

Because there is no place like home, it has special tax treatment.

- Any capital gain made when you sell your home is generally not taxed. If you have two houses in the U.K., you can choose which of them is your main home for CGT. By swapping backwards and forwards, combined with careful use of exemptions, a person with two houses may avoid CGT altogether. It makes up for all that gardening and housework.

- If you borrow money to buy a house, some of the interest may be tax deductible (though in the U.K., MIRAS relief was first drained away and then reclaimed by the government).

- In the U.K., letting rooms in your house can be tax free if the rent is less than a given limit. This is called **rent-a-room** relief, but requires a legitimate tenant. Use by the hour might constitute a brothel. Despite being illegal, keeping a disorderly house is fully taxable.

- Going away and letting your whole house can be very tax efficient. In the U.K., all your mortgage interest plus a range of expenses are deductible from rental income. Again, with the right timing, it is possible to avoid any CGT when you sell the house, even if you have hardly lived in it yourself.

- Letting out one house while living in another is another good ruse, especially if the let property is a **holiday home**, to which especially generous tax reliefs apply. This ensures plenty of weekend holiday cottages for flexi-time Inspectors who can leave work before the rush hour.

TAX PLANNING

People feel about tax the way they feel about sex. They are afraid they are missing out and that if they knew the right secrets they could do better: they could protect their money from the taxmen.

Like all myths, it is partly true.

Minimising tax is 1% destiny and 99% design. It is destiny to be born in the Cayman Isles, with no income tax, corporation tax, or inheritance tax. All the rest is planning: either off-the-shelf planning, culled from articles in Sunday newspapers, or expensive, bespoke, designer planning. But both are hopeless without one thing: money. Tax planning is not alchemy. If you have no money to start with you only have two choices:

1. Play with the benefits system instead.

2. Become a tax adviser and sell ideas to other people. Later on, when you have practised with their money, you can play the game with your own.

All tax planning should carry the warning: 'Don't let the tax tail wag the dog.' In other words, do not do something only for tax reasons. If you do, you may make the wrong decisions and lose more than you save in tax.

When playing at this level of the tax game, there are bonus points for:

- **Black holes**: areas of the board where you can place money but no-one can tax it. Profits which two countries both incorrectly believe has been taxed by the other have slipped down a black hole.

- **Loopholes**: faulty links in tax legislation which allow you legally to avoid tax.

To win at this game, you need **tax reclaims** and **tax shelters**; to win significantly, try **tax exile**; to hit the jackpot, use **international tax structures**.

Tax Reclaims

All governments are holding billions of pounds in over-collected tax. Although some periodically attempt to tell taxpayers this, we suspect them of bluffing, as the excess comes in useful when balancing the books.

The first step in tax planning is thus simple: check whether the government has any of your money. Then demand its immediate release, with tax-free interest as compensation for its wrongful imprisonment.

The source of these overpayments will vary by time and country. But it is worth reviewing the following:

- **Bank and building society interest**. Tax is commonly deducted from interest before you receive it, although non-taxpayers can ask for interest to be paid gross. In many cases people never get round to filling in the relevant form, so tax continues to be deducted from the interest before payment. This can be reclaimed.

- **The PAYE system**. This spreads tax allowances, such as the personal allowance, evenly through the year. Any break in employment may mean too much tax has been deducted during the tax year. Moving countries part-way through a tax year can have the same effect. A reclaim may help fund your round-the-world trip.

- **Income from overseas**. If this has suffered foreign tax and also been taxed in your home country, you may be entitled to recover the second tax paid.

  You may also be entitled to tax reliefs and allowances in the overseas country. For example, a Frenchman with a U.K. rental property is eligible for a U.K. personal allowance, which may allow him to recover tax deducted from the rental income. This shows real savoir faire.

Tax Shelters

Tax shelters are like buses. They come past occasionally, sometimes in groups. Their timetable depends on the generosity (or the lethargy) of the government. If you don't jump on when one comes by, you may have missed the last bus and have to pay tax.

Eventually you have to get off, and your money may then become taxable. Clever planners hop on another bus as it rounds the corner, and thus delay paying tax for the duration of the next ride. Keep changing buses like this, and you might die in the passenger seat and avoid tax altogether.

Before hailing a passing tax shelter, check the fare. Charges levied by the shelter's managers may mean it is only good value if you are a higher rate taxpayer. Ask yourself: 'Can I afford to travel first-class?'

Each country has its own tax shelters. In the U.K. they include:

(until recently) **TESSAs** (Tax Exempt Special Savings Accounts). This was an adults-only investment, and the door is now closed to new members. Those already in the club can transfer their funds to Tessa's cousin, **TOISA** (Tessa Only Individual Savings Account).

PEPs (Personal Equity Plans). Any gains are tax free. But charges may outweigh the benefits and, if the PEP falls in value, there is no tax relief for the loss.

ISAs (Individual Savings Accounts). The offspring of PEP and TESSA, these hold a wide mix of assets — **isa** bit of this and **isa** bit of that. Like the fearsome children of mythology, ISAs have devoured their parents.

National Savings Certificates. Government savings
products which pay tax-free interest in exchange
for you trusting politicians with your money. But
remember to withdraw it if a world war is
announced.

Pension Funds. Here, money is paid into a pension
fund gross, i.e. before being taxed, and once in the
fund it also grows tax free. This makes it a tax
shelter. Salesmen, who are trained to bluff, will say
this often and very plausibly. But remember that
you will pay tax on most of it when you retire, and
that dividends (which are a major part of the
income of a pension fund) are taxed before receipt.
So it's more of a lean-to than a shelter.

Tax Exile

Tax has traditionally been territorial, because it is
easier to collect money from people who live locally.
Tax also overrides ethnic origins: a German who moves
to France is caught by the French tax system.

The few exceptions to this apply whenever a
government thinks it can get away with it. The U.S.
Internal Revenue Service, for example, taxes all citizens
wherever they live, using its infernal computer
system, and withdraws citizenship if they don't
submit. Other nations tax any assets left behind
when you go abroad. But in general this principle of
territoriality means that going overseas can reduce
your tax bill, or even eliminate it altogether. Before
you cross the border consider:

Dates. Exactly when you go abroad can make an
enormous difference. Most countries work on a

calendar year basis, but the U.K.'s tax year starts on 6 April. Leaving the day before may save you a fortune.

Definitions. The precise definition of 'resident' varies by country, and some have different definitions depending on the tax you are considering. In the U.K. you may be non-resident for income tax but resident for capital gains. In Austria, having a ski apartment may make you tax resident. Discovering this too late may cause a crevasse in your financial arrangements. If you keep moving, you may be tax resident nowhere. A rolling stone may gather no moss, but it can acquire a certain polish – and a tax free lump sum.

Destination. Don't jump out of the chip pan into the French frier. Check the tax regime in the new country before you land. Simple steps, like closing bank accounts, may make a big difference to your tax bill.

Death. The tax you pay on death may depend on domicile rather than residence. Your domicile is your original home, and it can only be changed with difficulty. Thus a Kiwi backpacker remains domiciled in the Antipodes even if he spent the last two years studying reincarnation in Tibet.

Your country of domicile may also tax your worldwide assets when you die, even though you went abroad decades before. Countries which operate a domicile system are extremely reluctant to believe anyone might choose to live anywhere else. Buying a cemetery plot overseas is, however, accepted as reasonable evidence that you don't intend to come back – at least not this lifetime.

Artificial Tax Planning Schemes

Traditional tax specialists advise clients on efficient tax planning. Others, often merchant banks, sell artificial schemes. These are more risky, much better rewarded, and provoke the taxmen.

It is, in practice, easy to spot an artificial scheme:

- It comes with lots of jargon, mathematical diagrams and at least two legal opinions.

- The only really clear part of the documentation is the amount of money which the scheme will save, and the bank's share of this.

- It will be proprietary. This means that you won't be told anything about it until you've signed a confidentiality agreement, promising not to discuss it with anyone who might help you understand.

It is vital to realise that the team from the bank are all salesmen. The originator has been left behind in the bank's back office, where he can put his talents to better use dreaming up the next scheme.

You will keep control of the situation if you ask:

- Has the scheme been sold to anyone else? You need to know what your competitors are doing.
- Does it rely on invisibility for its success? It won't be secret for long if they have already discussed it with 18 companies.
- What are the indirect tax implications? Merchant banks often overlook transaction taxes as they are seen as less sexy than direct taxes.
- What is the downside risk? This will make them anxious in case you understand the scheme. You

need to know the risk because if it goes wrong someone's going to get the blame. Don't let it be you.
- What sort of guarantees can you give me that this
will work?

Some countries require that schemes are pre-
registered with the tax authorities, so that buyers
have to put the registered number on their tax
returns. This is the tax equivalent of jogging past a
police station carrying a sack labelled 'swag': you are
bound to be stopped and questioned.

INTERNATIONAL TAX

All tax is a game, but international tax is a top-level,
multi-dimensional game, played for high stakes: you
can win or lose millions. Its aim is to move money
round the world so most of it ends up in the hands of its
owners, and as little as possible leaks out on the way.

The game is played with five variables: **Vehicles**,
Passengers, **Havens**, **Networks** and **Residences**.
Because of the number of options, a tax planning
structure is like a kaleidoscope. You must keep your
eye on the moving patterns. For example:

- The profitability of an enterprise may not turn out
as expected.
- Corporate objectives may alter.
- The law in one of the countries may change.

This need for constant review provides international
tax experts with a regular income. They also have to
make regular trips abroad, especially to sunny tax
havens.

1. Vehicles

To move money around you need get-away vehicles. Rollers or rollerblades, boats or balloons: the choice is yours. The skill lies in picking the one best suited to your purpose: don't buy a mountain bike if you need a four-wheel drive. Forms of transport include:

Companies

These are the Ford Fiestas of international planning: universally popular, simple to operate and relatively cheap. They are therefore unlikely to attract much attention; the authorities do not pull them over unless they really misbehave.

Unlike cars, companies reproduce. Parent companies produce children, or **subsidiaries**. Each subsidiary is a separate person, but linked by share ownership to its parent.

Companies are nearly always taxed on their profits by the country in which they are resident. Residence is a separate variable in its own right.

Branches

Branches are not separate legal entities, but remain attached to the parent tree. In international tax terms this means that a branch belongs both where it is situated and where its parent is resident. For example, a French branch of an Australian company is part of the Australian company, so its profits will be taxed in Australia. But the French will also regard it as taxable in France.

This is unhelpful if the branch is profitable, but can be useful if it makes losses. If your company is setting up overseas for the first time, suggest that it begins as a branch, so start-up losses can be used by the main company. It can then convert to a subsidiary once it begins to make profits. With any luck, an idea like this will at least get you a couple of free trips abroad, allegedly to check that the proposal works in practice.

Rep(resentative) offices
Like many other reps, these are capable only of superficial relationships. If they show any sort of commitment, they immediately have to resign and become something more respectable, like a branch.

Lots of companies use reps in places with difficult or expensive tax regimes, like China. The advantage of reps is that they do not pay tax, because they are not supposed to be doing any real work.

Partnerships
If companies are parents, and reps are casual seducers, partnerships fall somewhere between the two. Partners generally define what they expect of one another rather than this being laid down by law. One of the partners can be a **sleeping partner**. This means the only business involvement is providing cash – e.g., paying the hotel bills. **Silent partners** are sleeping partners whose identity cannot be disclosed. They are thus ideal for secret affairs.

Partnerships often have no separate status in law: any tax falls on the partners as individuals. However some more enlightened countries, such as Holland, have formalised the arrangements and recognise partnerships as separate legal entities.

The fact that partnerships are seen as groups of individuals by some countries and as separate legal entities by others can be very useful. It is like a two-way mirror: the tax authorities abroad may see a German limited partnership as a group of individuals, and tax them accordingly; the German government taxes the same people as a single legal entity. The word for this sort of structure is **hybrid**. As with gardening, judicious use of hybrids is more fruitful than using only simple corporate offshoots.

2. Passengers

Some passengers are always stopped at the border. Others slip out unnoticed, hidden discreetly under the back seat or disguised as legitimate cargo.

Money is your passenger, but it travels in many guises. Its costume determines how much can be moved, and how easily. Knowledge of its 'wrappers' is useful, if only to show that you are really familiar with money in all its forms, and can be trusted to handle a lot more of it. They include:

Dividends. This is the most up-front way of taking money out of a company. Tax authorities are familiar with dividends and will tax them. Sometimes this tax will fall on the shareholder, sometimes on the company, and in the worst cases, on both.

Interest. If a business borrows money from abroad, it usually pays interest to the overseas lender. Note that this interest is deducted from profits before tax. Thus, if the lender is another entity within the same group, paying interest may be a way of getting money out without paying foreign tax on it.

Taxmen tore their hair out over this for a while, and finally introduced **thin cap** rules, which restricted the amount of inter-company interest that could be deducted from profits for tax purposes. This legislation has now been abolished in the U.K., as part of a wider non-discrimination policy sponsored by balding Eurocrats.

Taxmen may also take **withholding tax** from the interest. This means they keep back, or withhold, a slice of the interest as it slips over the border.

Interest nevertheless remains a useful tax-planning tool. Asking, "How much debt can we get away with?" will show that you understand this, while recognising the limitations.

Royalties, copyrights and know-how. If an overseas entity uses your software, publishes your book or develops your ideas, you can charge for it. This payment is deductible before tax, and provides another way of moving pre-tax profits abroad.

But a sharp tax inspector can spot a royalty at twenty miles. He will probably impose a withholding tax, and may also ask whether it is reasonable to make the payment at all.

There is a knack to using royalties, copyrights and know-how, and it is this: never be greedy. Sliced thinly and layered over interest and dividends they make tasty morsels for international corporate treasuries.

Management charges. The costs of running your complex group, with its companies, branches, partnerships and rep offices has to be paid for. Apart from anything else, your salary will be too much for any one entity to bear on its own. It will also be easier to camouflage if spread around.

Most tax authorities accept that head-office or management charges can legitimately be shared out among the group. Your aim is to put most of the charges in the country with the highest tax rate, where they will reduce the taxable profits; the taxmen will want the opposite. Good luck.

Transfer pricing. This is the hardest area for taxmen to pin down, and the most sophisticated way of stripping profits out of a country. If you sell goods or services to a sister company overseas, at what price do you sell them? Since 'profit' is sale price less cost, cost can determine profit. If you send the goods to India (a high tax country), via Bermuda (a low tax country), the goods may be sold to Bermuda cheaply, and then on-sold to India at a high price. This traps much of the profit in Bermuda en route.

Transfer pricing is the modern battleground, the tax Armageddon. No more duelling at dawn with gentlemanly Inspectors. Moving millions, even billions, of profit across borders requires a sophisticated Revenue defence system, like cruise missiles. Like most cruises, a transfer pricing investigation is both unhurried and expensive. Its cost, in professional fees alone, can blow a huge hole in a well-planned budget.

If you work for a large multinational, you will one day have a transfer pricing investigation. Here are a few survival tips:

a) Prepare your defences. If you work in sales or finance, make sure that either you were not responsible for setting the prices, or that you can defend them.

b) Know your enemy. For example, do not mess with the IRS. The U.S. Internal Revenue Service does not take prisoners. On the other hand, some countries' transfer pricing teams make Inspector Clouseau look professional.

c) Recruit more troops. This always helps, especially when you want to go home early or have a day off. Recruiting is much cheaper than paying outside advisers, and thus easily justified.

40

Do not let the hit-squads deter you completely. Done well, transfer pricing can still be an effective way of managing international tax.

Withdrawal. As always, this is a method of last resort, and tends to be messy. Companies can be liquidated, branches closed down and partnerships dissolved. But withdrawal will be expensive in real terms, such as property and legal costs. And the foreign government will make one last heroic effort to tax you before departure.

The golden rule is: look before you leap. Spend a little money on market research before you invest in a country, rather than a fortune in legal fees and tax costs when you leave.

3. Tax Havens

Tax havens are mostly sunny islands like Barbados. They keep your money safe for ever – or at least until the revolution. The locals, who earn peanuts nailing shelf company nameplates to solicitors' doorways, will one day want their share of the wealth.

Tax authorities in developed countries dislike havens, and have tried to limit their use. Most have introduced **anti-avoidance** legislation aimed at companies who set up tax haven subsidiaries. The U.K. Revenue call such subsidiaries Controlled Foreign Companies or **CFCs**, and believe they are more environmentally damaging than spray cans.

While all havens are guilty of 'harmful tax competition', some also stand accused of a more heinous offence – washing the ill-gotten gains of criminals through anonymous accounts. The U.K. decided to set a good example. It requires everyone, from pensioners to priests, to prove their identity before opening a bank account, in case they are money laundering for the Mafia. Bluffers should be scornful of this burdensome bureaucracy. Smugglers have utility bills too.

4. Networks

A world wide web predates the Internet. Money and wealth are transferred around the globe via an invisible network of international tax treaties. The number of treaties possessed by each country varies: some countries are treaty-rich and some treaty-poor. Outlaw countries have no treaties at all.

Tax treaties include clauses on some or all of the following:

- Agreement on how key concepts, such as residence, are defined.
- **Double tax relief (DTR)**. Sadly, not double relief from tax. DTR prevents you being taxed in both countries on the same money.
- Reduced withholding tax on interest, dividends, royalties, and similar.
- Exchange of information. The taxmen on both sides will co-operate to catch you.

Tax havens are outlawed from this treaty system. There are no tax treaties with the Cayman Islands or Panama. This is because treaty countries do not want to make it even easier for their citizens to do business in such low tax areas.

There are however a few invaluable tax haven countries which link into the network via one or two treaties. Good tax planning uses these connections to move money to a tax haven. Finding the best sequence of treaties to effect this transfer is called **treaty-shopping**.

On your next visit to Amsterdam, discard your inhibitions and order a **Dutch sandwich**: not three in a bed, but classic treaty-shopping. The Netherlands has a large network of tax treaties. It is relatively easy to get your money to Holland, using one of the many available treaties. The country also has a treaty with its colonial offspring, the Netherlands Antilles, which is a tax haven. Once you have moved your money to Holland, you can use the Netherlands Antilles treaty to take it out again, virtually tax free.

5. Residence

If you play games with residence, remember that countries define it in different ways. The two main ones are:

1. A company is resident where it is incorporated. For example, a company set up under Mexican law is resident in Mexico.

2. A company is resident where it is managed and controlled, i.e., where the company's key decisions are made. Unlike incorporation, 'management and control' is not a black and white issue. Never forget that tax planners' favourite colour is grey.

By passing both tests, i.e., being incorporated in one and managed and controlled in another, a company can be **dual resident**, which means it is regarded as tax resident in both countries. This can have advantages: for example there may be a double deduction for expenses or interest paid, called **double-dipping**. It is more difficult (but not impossible) to fail both tests, so that the company is not resident anywhere.

But if your aim is to be offshore, it is no good spending a fortune setting up a Bermudan resident company when the directors have board meetings in a hotel at Heathrow. If they do, the company will be deemed to be managed and controlled in Britain. The directors will just have to be self-sacrificing, put the company first, and travel to Bermuda on a regular basis.

TAX PROFESSIONALS

Personalities

Tax experts belong to one of three personality types:

Zealots who believe all the rules. In the Middle Ages they would have been theologians. Today most join the Inland Revenue or Customs & Excise.

Machiavellians who plan complicated ways around the rules and are regarded as heretics by zealots. In an earlier century they would have been burnt at the stake.

Pragmatists who negotiate practical solutions to tax problems. This is much the smallest group and should be cherished, if you are ever fortunate enough to meet one.

New recruits to the tax trade must get used to admitting in public what they do for a living. The simple statement, 'I'm a tax specialist,' can put an end to the liveliest conversations and produce silences in pubs. This is because the public never expects to meet certain kinds of people, such as nuns or tax specialists, in a normal social environment. They will be particularly worried if you work for the Revenue or Customs.

Although it is possible to dissemble and invent a fictitious profession, perpetrators are quickly discovered. Fake airline pilots are unmasked as soon as they meet another pilot, who usually turns out to be the local District Inspector.

Tax people are generally perceived as divided by a barbed wire fence. On one side is the **Revenue** and **Customs**. On the other are **Tax Advisers** working for accountancy and legal firms or large companies. In reality people cross the fence surprisingly often, usually leaving the Revenue to join better-paid private-sector poachers.

Remember this fence-crossing before you insult the Revenue in front of your tax adviser – last week he may have worked for them. Some of his best friends will still be Tax Inspectors. Otherwise, how would he gain the inside knowledge you are paying him for?

Inland Revenue

A good Inspector and a bright professional adviser relate to each other like First World War flying aces and their opposite numbers. This is as close as most tax specialists get to being a pilot. The Inland Revenue is an enemy, but one worthy of respect.

This is partly because of their rigorous Civil Service training. It would be unkind to say that Inspectors are those who are left behind when MI5 have picked out the best and brightest. But many are secret agents manqué, loving the thrill of undercover investigation – even if it is only fraud and false accounting in a Chinese takeaway.

Tax cases are a key part of an Inspector's training. Inspectors know hundreds, even thousands, of cases. One of the highest accolades in the Revenue is to get your name on a major case so the next generation have to learn it. Rarer still is the Revenue equivalent of the Cheltenham double, seen in *Stokes v. Costain* and *Ensign Tankers [Leasing] Ltd v. Stokes*. Less successful Inspectors buy personalised number plates.

There are many advantages to employing an ex-Inspector. He will have lots of practical experience, and great contacts. But he may want to go home at five, and at noon on Fridays.

Customs & Excise and the CA

Customs' first responsibility is to catch smugglers. They may need a reminder that legitimate VAT planning arrangements are not in the same league.

Customs are less intellectual than the Revenue, and survive on a diet of internal leaflets. In some cases their knowledge is thin to the point of anorexia. If you read the legislation, you may surprise them.

Collecting National Insurance Contributions used to be carried out by a branch of the DSS called the Contributions Agency. But the CA was outmanoeuvred by the professionals: in 1998 the Inland Revenue staged a successful takeover, brandishing the weapons of greater efficiency and cost savings.

As in most revolutions, the defeated did not disappear, but survive as moles within the Revenue structure. They are involved in the wily plot to re-label benefits as 'Working Tax Credits'. In reality these tax credits have nothing to do with tax at all, but are simply handouts masquerading as tax reliefs. They are part of a dastardly plan hatched by ex-DSS officers to make people work for their benefits instead of child-minding, cooking, cleaning and watching daytime TV.

Tax Advisers

Most firms of lawyers and accountants employ tax specialists: it is cheaper than buying the skills outside. Some advisers work on their own, as sole practitioners, or gather together in pairs or packs called partnerships.

Most professional firms are hierarchical, which means only partners get offices and the rest are open-plan. The hierarchy includes:

Tax Partner: Spends most of his time keeping clients happy rather than reading new rules, so is an inveterate bluffer.

Tax Group Manager: Draws lines for trainees to keep their toes on, takes them out for drinks and checks timesheets.

Tax Manager: Workhorse. The fiscal equivalent of the AA; ring them up and they'll rush round with a copy of the Taxes Acts. Make sure you have their mobile phone number.

Tax Senior: Learning to be a workhorse, dreaming of being a partner.

Tax Trainee: Experts in time-management, spend three years balancing professional exams with plans for post-qualification peregrinations.

Tax Accountants in industry are sometimes recruited by the professional firms, but they tend to introduce fresh air and raise clouds of dust. On the other hand, tax people often travel in the opposite direction and move from the profession to companies. This is like leaving a convent: few return to the habit.

Buying Tax Advice

Although it is generally illegal to practice as a lawyer, doctor or auditor without the relevant qualifications, in many countries any bluffer can set up as a tax specialist. If you need a job, this is perfect. If you need advice, stage a beauty parade. Look for:

- **A slimline organisation**. Too much fat finds its way into the fees.

- **Previous experience**. Virgins have to learn on the job and this is expensive.

- **Long term potential**. The relationship has to survive as you change and grow.

- **Last minute substitutions**. The attractive charismatic partner moves on to the next client.

Another way of assessment is to compare the adviser to a geographer. The latter does not know every detail about a country, but he knows the lie of the land.

The same is true of a good tax specialist. He may not have done any inheritance tax for years, but he knows that if you want to put some money into an offshore trust, this raises complex tax issues. In other words, he has a tax atlas in his head. When you ask a question he knows the location of the answer, if not its postcode. He will also tell you if he does not know the answer. Always remember that you are the bluffer.

When aeroplanes crash, rescuers look for the black box. Company directors may treat tax in the same way, and wait till something goes wrong before getting involved. Be different. Try asking:

- For a summary of the tax consequences for all major transactions.
- What the cost will be. This will be good news for most advisers, who waste hours later on trying to extract fees. Since the cost of this time is frequently added to the next bill, agreeing an estimate up-front immediately reduces this overhead.
- Whether there is an alternative. Tax people are always saying they are creative: let them prove it.

Accounting for Tax

There is only one essential fact to remember about Tax Accounting. It is not tax. It is an estimate of the tax payable which is included in the year end accounts.

Because it's not tax, tax specialists tend to look down on it. Although they send company accounts to the tax office, these are accompanied by a return or computation which calculates the tax payable on a more exact basis. In the past neither tax specialists nor the Revenue worried too much why the accounts tax charge was twice as big as the number in the computation. But the Inspector has got wise to this, and recruited real accountants to help. Letters from the Revenue can now contain seriously difficult accounting questions. If your adviser looks worried, ask him if there is a GAAP in his knowledge. Put simply, there are two common reasons why the numbers are so different:

1. Lots of borderline reliefs and exemptions have been deducted in your computation, but the Inspector may realise they are borderline and challenge them. Accountants, being prudent, insist on these being ignored for the accounts.

2. Some items can be deducted immediately in the accounts, but must be spread for tax purposes. This is called a **timing difference**. Accounts have to be adjusted for timing differences, and this is done by setting up artificial or **deferred** tax. Deferred tax is irreconcilably difficult. Defer to the specialists: it is their job to balance the books.

Profit before tax (PBT) is the accountants' revenge for being despised by tax specialists. Accountants believe tax is a fixed cost, and thus it is the profit before tax which reflects how well the organisation has performed against competitors. Worse, they have persuaded market analysts that this is true.

This view is deeply insulting to tax specialists, whose lives are dedicated to reducing the tax charge. Calling tax a fixed cost undermines the specialists' whole raison d'être, and devalues their contribution to a company's profitability.

Concentrating on profit before tax to the exclusion of the actual tax paid can be very costly. Accountants who deal with fictitious rolling budgets and round sum estimates often forget that tax paid leaves the company's coffers for ever. It cannot be adjusted next year like an accounting entry.

Actuaries are even worse than accountants at this. They live in an arcane area called a reserve, to which access is restricted. In these enclosures they play with huge artificial numbers, completely losing touch with everyday realities, such as cash.

UNDERSTANDING TAX LAW

Most religions are split into two factions. One follows the text of the scriptures, interpreting its exact words and comparing them internally, rather like literary criticism. The other seeks to express the heart of the religious message, and sees the scriptures as helpful, but not ultimately authoritative.

Taxation is similarly divided between those who follow the words of the legislation and others who try to discover what the legislation was intended to do. We can call the first the literal school and the second the purposive school.

The U.K. and most of its ex-colonies follow the first approach. Europe generally takes a more purposive line. Both have advantages and disadvantages. The literal approach gives greater certainty: if the law says X then X will apply. The disadvantage is that making X apply in these circumstances may be nonsense, and clearly not what Parliament meant.

In either case, tax law can be sub-divided into rules. It is not always easy, however, to know which rules apply to you. This may be because your situation is unusual. But this is unlikely. The more probable reasons are that:

- You cannot find out what the rules are.
- You can find the rules but they are incomprehensible.
- The rules are not being followed in practice.

The core of U.K. law is parliamentary legislation or **statute law**. Its gaps are glossed over until someone gets into an argument with the Revenue and one or other of them takes a case to court. The decisions of the judges form **case law**.

If the Revenue loses a case, it has the power and influence to get the statute changed. Usually this type of change is accompanied by an announcement that the change 'puts the law back where everyone thought it was'.

Mostly this behaviour is tolerated, unless the Revenue announce that the new legislation is **retrospective**. This means that they have effectively unpicked the court's decision. Retrospection is generally regarded as overstepping the mark.

Even the Revenue recognise that tax law is a foreign language, and publish their interpretations as **Statements of Practice**. To top it all, government departments also issue **regulations**.

The tax rule on a particular point may thus be an amalgam of case law, statute, regulation and interpretation. This is why tax advisers cover their letters with caveats – nooks and crannies which provide protection if the roof falls in on their arguments.

Accessibility

If you want to solve a tax problem, knowing where to start is not easy. Even bluffers need a few facts to hide behind. We recommend:

- **Revenue pamphlets**. These have the advantage of being free, but the disadvantage that they won't point out any weaknesses in the taxman's case.

- **Tax annuals**. These are found in public libraries, NB: never read last year's annual. It's dangerous and can seriously damage your wealth.

- **Free literature**. Most major accounting and law firms publish free booklets highlighting changes to tax law. Call their head office and ask for the Publications Department. Make sure your name goes on the mailing list it keeps your phone bill down.

- **Revenue manuals**. As part of a campaign for open government, these can be found on the Revenue's web site. They include summaries of the government's approach to tax law and practice. But you won't find everything: they may be open but they're not wide open. The most interesting parts are hidden from outsiders. These patches are known to Inspectors as 'purple text' and describe in ornate detail how to trip up tax planners.

Taxspeak

Tax draftsmen have traditionally refused to use three sentences when one would do. For example:

> 'Where the relief to which a person is entitled for any year of assessment consists in an income tax reduction calculated by reference to a specified amount, the effect of that relief shall be that the amount of that person's liability for that year to income tax on his total income shall be the amount to which he would have been liable apart from that provision less whichever is the smaller of—
>   a) the amount equal to 10% of the specified amount;
>   b) the amount which reduces his liability to nil.'*

Finally, even the Revenue couldn't understand it. They set up teams of translators to convert fiscal law into simpler language. This has upset many elderly tax specialists, who used section numbers as signposts through the legislative jungle.

* Translation: Certain personal allowances create a 10% tax credit, but this cannot be repaid to an individual unless he or she has sufficient taxable income.

However, the tax rewrite only simplifies the language, not the regime itself. Bluffers need to remember that translation is not a talisman, and cannot make an opaque system transparent. Most tax rules remain impenetrable to all but the seriously intrepid, so the letters you receive may still be incomprehensible. If this happens, refer the Inspector to his own Complaints Manual. It's your right as a taxpayer to prefer plain vanilla English.

Forms

Tax and forms go together like eggs and spoons, stories and journalists. One is a necessary to extract the other.

There are so many tax forms that the only reasonable course of action is to ask: "Is there a separate form for that?" whenever something new comes up. The chances are there will be. By asking you will get a gold star for good behaviour, and make penalties less likely.

People who never have to fill in a tax form are enviable creatures, like thin people who never have to diet. Membership of this charmed circle is open only to those whose income has been fully taxed before receipt, such as salary paid under PAYE, and U.K. bank or building society interest.

The Revenue will send you a form if they think you have more tax to pay. But they are not the know-alls they would have us believe: their standard tool-kit does not yet include a crystal ball. So if you have received income which has not been fully taxed, you are not allowed to blame the taxman for not sending you a tax form. You have to ask for it, painful though this is.

Self Assessment

Britain has now been hectored into **SA**, or Self Assessment. Like self analysis and self help it originated in the U.S., although a similar system exists in Australia and France. SA also stands for Sex Appeal. The similarities are startling:

1. Both mark the passage from childhood to adulthood. Under SA, taxpayers take responsibility for their own returns: they can no longer blame their employer or the Revenue.

2. Despite hundreds of articles in the press, no-one really understands how either work.

3. Both carry risks and penalties, and cause unexpected misunderstandings.

4. In a thorough investigation, midnight raids occur.

However, while Sex Appeal depends on shape, Self Assessment depends on forms. These arrive in April. If you miss the 30 September cut-off date, you will have to fill in the forms and calculate the tax due. If you haven't done so, and paid the tax by the following 31 January, you will suffer interest and penalties.

The only way out is a 'reasonable excuse' such as life-threatening illness or burglars stealing your books of account. Pressure of work, ignorance, poverty or holidays abroad are no protection once you have entered the penalty zone.

But if you play their game and send the relevant information to the Revenue by 30 September, they will calculate your tax, and tell you what to pay, just as they did before. Although this Revenue calculation is also called Self Assessment, it is not. SA is thus an enormous Revenue bluff.

AVOIDING AND EVADING

It is important to distinguish avoiding tax from its evasion. The difference is the thickness of a prison wall.

Tax Avoidance

Tax avoidance means using the existing law to reduce your tax bill. The key principle is that no-one *'is under the smallest obligation, moral or other, so to arrange his legal relations to his business or to his property as to enable the Inland Revenue to put the largest possible shovel into his stores'*. This useful quotation comes from the case of *Ayrshire Pullman Motor Services & Ritchie v. CIR*.

If you organise your affairs so the Revenue have to use the smallest possible shovel, quote the case of *Duke of Westminster v. CIR*. In this the judge said that everyone *'is entitled if he can to order his affairs so that the tax attaching under the appropriate Acts is less than it otherwise would be'*.

You need to be aware, however, that this Westminster principle has its limitations, introduced because taxpayers, like teenagers, pushed the rules as far as they could. So elaborate were the avoidance schemes that the courts decided the Westminster principle would not apply if there were:

a) a pre-planned series of transactions
b) steps inserted into the transactions which had no business purpose other than tax avoidance.

When the Revenue know that you can legally avoid tax, they tend to introduce anti-avoidance legislation to prevent you. If something sounds too good to be true, ask: "What about anti-avoidance legislation?"

Even if you are told none exists, be warned: it can be introduced overnight and catch you with your fiscal trousers down.

Tax Evasion

Tax evasion means you have deliberately not paid tax. If you are found out, you will have to pay large sums of back tax, interest and penalties, and your file will be marked with a sticker saying, 'WATCH THIS ONE'. In the most serious cases, you may go to jail. This is not a bluff.

Investigation

It is very unpleasant to be investigated by the Revenue or Customs, especially if they suspect you of evasion. If you are being investigated, your first question is always 'Why?' These are some of the answers:

- You have been moonlighting, and advertised your skills in the local paper. The Revenue read it.
- You suppressed some cash takings from your business, and as a result your profits are lower than the taxman would expect. Both organisations have detailed studies for most types of business showing normal profits and the key variable factors.
- Something unusual in your tax return has prompted a tax official to ask questions.
- Taxmen have posed as customers, had dinner in your restaurant, then checked whether their payment went into your books. The food portions you served may also have been used as a statistical sample to see if the profit margin on the meal matches that in your accounts.

- Someone has sneaked on you.
- A bank has reported your savings interest to the Revenue. This is cross-checked to your tax return.
- Your lifestyle doesn't match your declared earnings.

As well as being investigated because of Revenue suspicions, you may also be the subject of a random audit. This means you have been selected on a statistical basis: a sort of reverse National Lottery.

The trouble is, no-one will tell you this, so you won't know whether the investigation is random or targeted. Keep records. You may need to prove where that money in your bank account came from.

At the other end of the spectrum from random audits, special investigation teams deal with the **Phoenix** and **Ghost**. This is not a real ale pub. A phoenix is a company which goes into liquidation, owing tax and VAT debts, and then starts up again under another company name. Ghosts are people who, as far as the tax office records are concerned, don't exist.

Justification

When called to see the taxman, the first reaction is to make excuses, such as:

- "I won the money in the lottery." This is so common that some countries have a black market in winning lottery tickets – after the winnings have been paid out to the original holder.
- "I won it on the horses." ('Show us your slips.')
- "I inherited it from an elderly distant aunt who lived abroad." ('Name her.')
- "It's just a hobby and I don't make much." ('How much?')

Do not try to argue that you should not be taxed because what you are doing is outside the law. In the tax case of *CIR v. Aken* a prostitute argued she could not be taxed because if she was, the Crown would be living on immoral earnings. She failed, presumably because the morality of most of the Crown's income has historically always been dubious.

Complaining

The Code requires the Revenue to reimburse your costs if they have made mistakes or been late getting back to you. Note that the Revenue idea of a delay is seven months – when they are writing the letters. If you take that long to reply, expect to be raided.

Mistakes include situations where the taxman has:

- Taken a 'wholly unreasonable' view of the law.
- Continued to ask questions about 'obviously trivial matters'.
- Ignored you when you corrected a Revenue mistake.
- Made a trivial mistake which could lead to far more serious consequences.
- Cannot stop making mistakes.

If this has happened to you, send the Revenue a bill for your expenses, including any lost earnings. You can also ask for a 'consolatory payment' as compensation for your distress.

The **Taxpayers' Charter** is a good scare tactic. It strikes terror into those who have not been 'fair, helpful, efficient and accountable' and is taken very seriously by Ministers. You may also wish to consider the **Revenue Adjudicator** whose sole purpose in life is to examine complaints from taxpayers and recommend solutions. Asking for the Adjudicator's address from your local Inspector may help focus his mind.

Negotiation

The Revenue wants you to pay tax and you object. Try negotiation: you may end up with a lower settlement. But it will only work if the Revenue believe you have something they want – apart, of course, from lots of tax.

Your objective is to persuade the Revenue that you are holding at least one of the following cards. Play them close to your chest:

- You believe there is some technical flaw in either the evidence itself or the Revenue interpretation of the evidence. Whether there is or not doesn't matter too much. If you can give a convincing display of your doubts, you may persuade a court.

- You will fight this case to the bitter end. Penniless debtors cannot pay tax. Also the DWP will be upset at the extra costs of maintaining your family.

- You will demand compensation and costs when you win. This will worry them. Their expense claim might be rejected by the Treasury. Worse still, it might go on their P11D.

- You have some information they want, perhaps on how a tax avoidance scheme works. If you tell them, they will save investigation time and can move on to the next case.

- If you settle the tax now, they'll have it by the end of March. This is the end of the Revenue's financial year. Taxmen have performance targets too.

GLOSSARY

Assessment – What you think of the Revenue.

ATII – Abbreviation for: a) member of the Chartered Institute of Taxation; b) 'All Tax Is Impossible', 'All Tax Is Impenetrable' and 'Any Tax Is Immoral'.

Back Duty – Investigation of unpaid tax. More painful than a slipped disc.

Benefits in kind – Earnings paid in goods rather than cash. Used to be kind to the pocket, but now so only at the margin; thus 'fringe' benefits.

Bond – Written acknowledgement of a loan to a company, which can be sold on the stock market. Bonds usually have numbers for security reasons, hence 007.

Bond washing – Tax avoidance device for turning income into capital gains by selling the bond before interest is received. The interest is thus included in the gain rather than being taxed as income. Effective bond-washing allows you to clean up.

Bracket creep – Tendency to be pushed into the next tax band by inflation, rather than because of increased real income. (Sycophantic inspectors recognise this but prefer to hide it in parentheses.)

Captive – Bank or insurance subsidiary company in a tax haven. The Revenue may hold the parent hostage until some profits are released.

Charge – The sudden and rapid collection of a tax. Avoidance may be fatal, as in the Charge of the Light Brigade.

Concession – Relaxation of the law in your favour, unless you're a tax avoider. Concessions never give rights to a gold mine.

Connected persons – Most relatives of a taxpayer, plus maids, but excluding lovers and mistresses.

Customs – First cousins of the Revenue, so-called because of their strange habits.

Day – 24 hours ending at midnight. A visit to the U.K. beginning at 9 a.m. and ending at 5 p.m. the same day is thus deemed never to have happened.

Death – The only other great certainty, now undermined by cryogenics.

Deem – Revenue-speak for 'Let's pretend'.

Discovery – The Inspector finds something new, which allows him to dig into your tax affairs.

Distress – Customs seize your goods. Very upsetting.

Excise – To take out. What happens if you get on the wrong side of your VAT Inspector.

Flip-flops – Clever tax avoidance schemes involving trusts. Could come undone if not properly secured.

Gross – Paid before deduction of tax, or excessive tax.

Interest – Shown by the Revenue if you don't declare all your bank accounts.

MIRAS – Greek God who nibbles at tax reliefs until they're invisible to the naked eye.

Net – Payment after deduction of tax. Previously used for fishing smuggled goods out of ponds. Customs today prefer muckraking to moonraking.

Offshore – Any country where the tax is less than at home. Regarded as offside by the Revenue.

Paradis fiscal – French for tax haven.

PAYE – Pay All You Earn.

PILON – Payment In Lieu of Notice; can give the redundant a high-voltage tax shock.

Ring fence – Separate and isolate for tax purposes. Similar to ring roads which separate drivers from their destination and isolate town centres.

Tax credit – a chameleon. Perhaps a benefit, perhaps a tax, perhaps a relief from tax.

Tax holiday – Period of freedom from tax.

Tax reliefs – What some people collect in the belief that they will ensure eternal life for their wealth, like medieval indulgences.

Tax Year – One which begins in the U.K. on 6 April and ends on the following 5 April. Caused by a historical accident when some days were irretrievably lost.

Tolls – Unexpected taxes, as in: 'it tolls for thee'.

Umbrella – A way of sheltering your unit or investment trusts from bad weather. An umbrella fund has many little funds sheltering beneath it, and you can swap from one to another. Watch out for the ill winds of Capital Gains Tax and Stamp Duty Reserve Tax.

Will – Strong intention to proceed. Where there's a will, there's a way of reducing death duties.

Winding-up – a) Method, such as tax planning, of dealing with the Revenue; b) unfortunate end to a business.

THE AUTHOR

A.J. Carroll hated school. He was hopelessly short-sighted, and thus always last to be picked for team games. Many years later, after university and a spell of teaching, he discovered tax. Finally, he had found a game he could play, enjoy and win.

He has spent fifteen years as a tax adviser, including three in the Far East, a long way offshore. Back home his clients have included a sculptress, an international bank and a breakfast cereal manufacturer. He has now taken shelter with a firm of professional accountants in the City of London.

Along the way he has collected four obscure languages, which comes in useful when translating taxspeak. When he is not dreaming of travel or tax, he writes romantic fiction. He claims this helps him maintain a grasp on reality.
